Here's what people have to say abou
Book Ser

I can't continue without saying it o
Muslim Girls! No damsels in distress, i
no cliché girly nonsense! ... This is exactly what our girls need to grow
up reading.
–Emma Apple, author of best-selling 'Children's First Questions'
Series

Learning about Islamic history and famous Muslims of the past makes
these books a historical book lover's wish, and the Islamic twist is a
plus for young Muslim readers. Jannah Jewels has been Muslimommy
approved as kid-friendly!
-Zakiyya Osman, MusliMommy.com

I love all of the Jannah Jewels books, and the fact that you combine
history and adventure in your stories. I also liked that you put the
holy verses of Quran that remind us to stay close to Allah and I liked
the fact that in one book you mentioned the verse from Quran which
mentions the benefit of being kind to your enemy. I have read all of
the Jannah Jewels books and even read two of these books in one day,
that's how much I like these books!
–Fatima Bint Saifurrehman, 8 Years Old

I could really feel the love that went into this book – the characters,
the places, the history, and the things that the author clearly strongly
believes in and wants to share with our children and the wider world
through her heroines…My daughter's verdict? "I would give the book
a 10 out of 10 mum"
–Umm Salihah, HappyMuslimah.com Blog

Fantastic book! My child was turning pages and couldn't wait to read
the next chapter. So much so he's asking for the next book in the series.
-Mrs. S. A. Khanom, Book Reviewer

By Umm Nura

Vancouver

*This book is dedicated to the wisdom and knowledge in China
and for my two little Jannah Jewels, Nura and Hanaan.*

Published by Gentle Breeze Books, Vancouver, B.C., Canada

Copyright 2013 by Umm Nura
Illustrations by Nayzak Al-Hilali

Visit us on the Web! www.JannahJewels.com

ISBN: 978-0-9867208-3-3

April 2013

Contents

Sport:

Archery

Role:

Guides and leads the girls

Superpower:

Intense sight and spiritual insight

Fear:

Spiders

Special Gadget:

Ancient Compass

Carries:

Bow and Arrow, Ancient Map, Compass

HIDAYAH

JAIDE

Sport:

Skateboarding

Role:

Artist, Racer

Superpower:

Fast racer on foot or skateboard

Fear:

Hunger (She's always hungry!)

Special Gadget:

Time Travel Watch

Carries:

Skateboard, Sketchpad, Pencil, Watch

Sport:

Horseback Riding

Role:

Walking Encyclopedia,
Horseback Rider

Superpower:

Communicates with
animals

Fear:

Heights

Special Gadget:

Book of Knowledge

Carries:

Book of Knowledge, has
horse named "Spirit"

IMAN

SARA

Sport:

Swimming

Role:

Environmentalist,
Swimmer

Superpower:

Breathes underwater for
a long time

Fear:

Drowning

Special Gadget:

Metal Ball

Carries:

Sunscreen, Water
canteen, Metal Ball

SUPPORTING CHARACTERS

JAFFAR

ZHENG HE

MASTER SWIMMER

THE JANNAH JEWELS ADVENTURE 2:

Nanjing, China

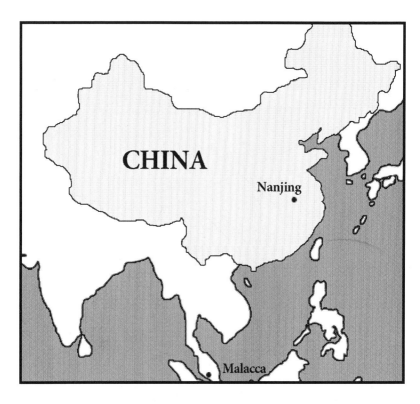

ARTIFACT 2: MEDICINAL PLANT IN MALACCA

"The more clear your heart is the easier it is to hit your target."

~Mother to Jaffar

Dear Reader, Assalamu'alaykum,

The world is waiting for peace and safety from the hands of Jaffar, who is still fast on the Jannah Jewels' trail. It was a close call in Timbuktu, West Africa. However, the Jannah Jewels worked hard, found the ancient manuscript and were victorious!

Now, the Jannah Jewels need to cross the mighty waters from China to find the next missing artifact for the Golden Clock. Along the way they will be faced with fiery arrows, scary pirates and raging waters!

Dear Reader, come join the adventure with your favorite characters Hidayah, Iman, Jaide and Sara and work together with the Jannah Jewels to help solve the mystery in Book Two, "The Chase in China".

May Peace be with you,
Umm Nura

Prologue

Long ago, there was a famous archer who mastered the way of the Bow and Arrow. He was given the enormous task of protecting the world from evil. He was a peaceful archer, who knew an important secret that made him extremely powerful; not only in archery but also in other ways you would not believe. The secret was written inside a scroll, placed in a box, and locked away inside a giant Golden Clock to be protected from the hands of evil.

But the Master archer was growing old, and the time had come to pass on his duty to an apprentice. He watched his students carefully every day. The students trained extra hard to earn the Master Archer's approval. Two students caught the Master Archer's eye: Khan and Layla. Khan was fierce in his fights, made swift strategies and had strong hands. Layla was flawless in her aim, light on her feet and had intense vision. Khan wanted to be the next master archer more than anything in the world. Layla, on the other hand, just wanted peace in the world, no matter who became the next Master

Archer. Finally, the day dawned when a new Master had to emerge. Despite everyone's surprise and for the first time in history, the duty was given to a girl—Layla. Layla trained relentlessly and over time proved her just and peaceful nature. The Master Archer said, "It is only the humble, the peaceful and those who can control their anger that are allowed to possess the secrets of the 'Bow and Arrow'."

Before long, Khan and Layla were married and practiced the way of the Bow and Arrow together. In time, they had two children, a boy named Jaffar and a girl named Jasmin.

Jaffar grew up to be a curious and gentle spirit who loved to practice calligraphy, read books, and sit for long hours under shaded trees. Jasmin, on the other hand, liked to play sports, tumble in the grass, and copy her mother in archery. They all lived peacefully together in the old, walled city of Fez in Morocco, *or so it seemed*.

Khan fought with Jaffar, his son, every day, urging him to work harder at archery. Had it been up to Jaffar, he would simply have sat for hours reading his books and practicing calligraphy. He was just not interested in archery, but his father was so fierce that Jaffar had no choice but to practice with his sister, Jasmin, who was a natural. As the days went on, trouble brewed, and gloom and misery settled upon the villa's walls. Over time, Jaffar grew to be an outstanding archer, fierce and powerful, much like his father, despite his not wanting to do so, and soon forgot all about his reading and writing. On the other hand, Layla practiced archery differently. She practiced to refine her skills and herself; she never used archery for fighting, but for strength-building and purifying her heart. Soon, this difference in practicing the Bow and Arrow caused problems for everyone.

*   *   *   *

Far away in Vancouver, Canada, Hidayah was sitting in her classroom, bored as usual. She had always thought that nothing exciting ever happened, but this day everything was about to change. Hidayah was walking home from school when she spotted a mysterious woman in the neighbourhood park. The woman was wearing dark red, flowing robes, and something behind her sparkled in the sunlight. It looked as though she were moving into the empty house on the hill. No one had ever lived there for as long as Hidayah could remember.

Hidayah decided she was done with being bored. So she started the long trek up to the house on the hill. She huffed up the porch stairs and tiptoeing, looked in one of the windows. She couldn't believe what she saw! It was the woman in long, dark red, flowing robes with a bow and arrow in her hands, standing so completely still that she looked like a wax statue. Her strong hands were wrapped around the bow, and her eyes were intently gazing at the target across the room. She was so focused and still that Hidayah had to hold her breath afraid of making any sound. Hidayah sat mesmerized waiting for the woman to let go of the arrow. *But she did not let go.*

So it happened that day after day, Hidayah would hurry up the hill to watch this mysterious woman. And every day she came closer and closer to the door of the house. Several months went by in this way until one day; Hidayah finally mustered enough courage to sit on the doorstep. Then, for the first time, the woman let go of the arrow, which landed in a perfect spot right in the center of the target. The woman turned and said, "So, you have come." She looked right into Hidayah's eyes as though she was looking through her. Hidayah, at first startled, regained her calmness and with her head lowered said, "My name is Hidayah, may I be your student? Can you teach me the Bow and Arrow?" And the woman replied, "I accepted you as my student the very first day you peeked through the window." Thus, Hidayah trained with the Master Archer for several years and was on her way to becoming a very strong, yet gentle, archer.

1

Sibling Rivalry

"Where is the artifact?!" shouted Khan.

Jaffar's face grew red and hot. His eyes were cast down. He wasn't able to return with the first artifact, the manuscript from Timbuktu. Hidayah and the Jannah Jewels were too clever and too fast for him.

"I tried to get it, and I was soo close, Father," said Jaffar. "But I saw it. I saw that Hidayah has the ancient compass."

"I knew it! Of course, she has it," shouted Khan. "You have to try harder next time, Jaffar. With all your practice and study of archery, you should be able to defeat her by now. The next archer who wins in the archery battle will take the throne."

"I know, Father, I know," said Jaffar.

"There are only a handful of people left who can win

that archery battle. Hidayah and you are the only strong candidates for it," said Khan. "That is why you must find the powerful secret in the Golden Clock that will reveal how to win the battle. You've got to find those artifacts before the Jannah Jewels!"

Jasmin, Jaffar's sister, was eavesdropping behind the curtains.

"I can beat her, Father. She is weak. She has lost her aim," said Jaffar.

"Apparently, so have you, Jaffar. You didn't come back with the artifact, did you?" said Khan.

Jaffar looked back on the floor. Suddenly, Jasmin came running out from behind the curtains, her bow and arrow bouncing behind her.

"Hello Father," said Jasmin, kissing him on the hand. "I am ready for my practice today."

Jasmin smiled sweetly at Jaffar, but with a hint of mischief glinting in her eye. She fixed her hijab and then carefully took her position. She stretched out the bow, looked intently at her aim, released her breath, and shot the arrow. It shot directly through an apple that was sitting on the pedestal *right* beside Jaffar.

"Your sister is becoming better at archery, Jaffar," said Khan. "Maybe *you* won't have to battle with Hidayah for the throne, after all."

"What do you mean?" asked Jaffar.

"He means that I can beat her, and I can be the next heir to the throne!" said Jasmin. "Oh, of course, I don't want anything to happen to you though, Father, I would miss you too much," said Jasmin. She smiled sweetly at her father. But when Khan's back was turned, she stuck out her tongue at her brother.

Jasmin wanted more than anything to become the next Master Archer. Jaffar was an excellent archer, but Jasmin knew that she was better. She was lighter on her feet, while Jaffar seemed heavy, not only in his feet but also in his heart. Mother used to say, "*To succeed in archery, you need a clear heart, as this shows in your aim. The more muddy your heart is, the harder archery becomes; and the more clear your heart is, the easier it is to hit your target.*" It seemed that Jasmin only wanted

8

to keep muddying Jaffar's heart.

"Jasmin, we will practice later tonight when I return from my Council meeting," said Khan.

"Can I come to this one, Father?" asked Jaffar.

"Ha!" Khan laughed. "No, you are still too young and need all the time in the world to keep practicing anyway." It looked like Khan was about to hug Jaffar, but as Jaffar stepped in closer, Khan just turned and walked away, while two of his assistants walked with him, one on either side.

"You're still *too* young," mimicked Jasmin, laughing at her brother. "Oh brother, when are you going to become a big man around here?"

"Leave me alone, Jasmin, I don't have time for this," said Jaffar.

"Oh, did I hurt your feelings, Jaffar, you poor thing," she cackled. "Why don't you just give up. You're never going to win. Besides, I'm getting better every day."

Suddenly, Jaffar got up and shot an arrow through a vase where Jasmin was resting her arm. Pieces of the vase shattered onto the floor. Jaffar sometimes lost his temper and broke things when he was mad. He didn't quite understand how to control his anger yet, but he was working on it. As soon as he heard the shattering of the vase, like the loudest moment of thunder striking, he remembered his mother reciting a hadith, a saying from the Prophet Muhammad, peace and blessings be upon him, "*A strong man is not he who defeats his opponent by wrestling, but a strong man is he who controls himself at the time of anger.*"

Relief spilled over him, like walking in cool, light rain as Jaffar's heart softened upon hearing the words of the Prophet in his heart. He wanted to control his anger more than anything; it's what his mother would have wanted. His mother used to tell him that it was okay to get angry because it's human to feel like that every once in a while, but it's how he released or transformed that anger that truly mattered.

Khan's assistants came rushing in to see what had happened.

Jaffar was about to speak up when Jasmin spoke before him, cutting him off mid-sentence.

"I'm so sorry, you know me, I'm still struggling with

this bow and arrow thing," said Jasmin.

"We will be telling your Father about this," said one assistant.

"You will help clean up this mess," said the other assistant.

Jaffar looked confused. *Why did Jasmin take the blame?*

"You owe me one, Brother," said Jasmin. Her arms were crossed and her eyebrows were knotted up.

Jaffar wondered what his sister was up to now. She was always scheming up tricks to play on her brother, even when Mother was still around.

Jaffar rested his bow and arrow against the wall and sat at the edge of the window. He pulled out his notebook and calligraphy pen set and began to write verses from the Qur'an, doing so always gave him peace. Today, as he looked out into the field, his eyes started to well up with tears.

"What's wrong with you *now*?" asked Jasmin. "I'm the one that's going to get in trouble and you're the one sobbing?"

"I miss Mother," said Jaffar. "Don't you? Don't you ever think about her?"

"No, I don't," lied Jasmin. "She never liked me anyway."

"That's not true, Jasmin, she loved both of us very much!" said Jaffar.

"Then why did she just *leave us*?" asked Jasmin.

"What do you mean, *leave us*?" said Jaffar. "She was sick and then she died—it's not her fault."

Jasmin looked flustered. She bit her lip and averted her eyes.

"Of course, uhm, yeah, she *died*, that's what I meant, *leave* us. I don't like to use the word *died*," mumbled Jasmin.

Jaffar knew his sister very well and knew when she was lying. His face grew that usual red and hot when he was about to lose his temper.

"What are you hiding from me?" he boomed, jumping to his feet. "What do you know?"

"Nothing, nothing!" said Jasmin. "Stop yelling at me."

"Jasmin! Tell me, right now!" shouted Jaffar.

"Fine, fine, okay, calm down," said Jasmin. Jasmin took out a carefully folded note from her pocket. "I'm sorry, Brother, I should have told you sooner," said Jasmin.

With his hands quivering, he sat down and opened up the note in his hands. He couldn't believe his eyes! It was a note from his mother that was written to him on the day he never saw her again. Jasmin had hidden the note from him all this time.

How could she do that?

Jasmin helped clean up the last remaining pieces of the shattered vase, then skipped, cartwheeled, and back-flipped down the hall.

"Sorry, Brother!" said Jasmin. "Don't forget, you owe me one!"

Tears poured down Jaffar's cheeks when he saw his mother's familiar penmanship, the style of calligraphy that he himself was trying to master.

"My mother... she's still alive!" whispered Jaffar. "I knew it."

2

The Letter

Suddenly, Khan entered the room. Jaffar quickly folded up the note and placed it into his pocket.

Father cannot learn that I know about this, thought Jaffar.

"What happened here?" said Khan. Jasmin was right behind him, hiding behind his long robes.

"He still needs all the practice he can get—he broke that vase!" said Jasmin.

Jaffar was incredulous.

"Oh, Jasmin, you don't have to be scared of Father. You can tell him what really happened," said Jaffar.

"Nooo, it was you!" said Jasmin.

"Excuse me, Jasmin. You just told us that *you* broke that vase," said Khan's assistant.

"Double duty out in the fields, Jasmin. One for breaking the vase and one for lying," said Khan. "I am disappointed in you."

Jasmin stormed off. She stared deep into Jaffar's eyes on her way out.

"I guess, I don't owe you one after all, Jasmin," said Jaffar.

"It's not over yet, Brother," said Jasmin. She motioned to the pocket where Jaffar had put the letter.

"Jasmin, c'mon, don't tell him--" motioned Jaffar.

She turned to Father.

"Father?" said Jasmin.

"What is it, Jasmin? Get going into the fields!" said Khan.

She looked back at Jaffar.

"Nah, I'll save this letter thing for another time," whispered Jasmin. "Ah, nothing Father, I'm going!"

Jaffar thought his shirt might get a hole in it; his

heart was beating so incredibly fast. He was so mad at Jasmin. The letter—it was his—Mother wrote it to *him*. He couldn't believe that his sister stole the letter and also kept it such a big secret. *Well, actually, he could kind of believe it.*

Even though most of the attention was always on Jaffar, the obvious heir to the throne, Jasmin had become quite skilled in archery. However, Jasmin wanted to prove everyone wrong, that girls could be the next heir to the throne based on skill and not gender. But the jealous tricks she pulled on Jaffar always got her into trouble. Her mother often scolded her and over time Jasmin became convinced that her mother didn't like her as much as she liked Jaffar. It might have been that Mother spent a lot of time with her brother, which didn't make sense to Jasmin at all. Her mother was a Master Archer and she wanted to be just like her mother, thinking it would make her mother happy. She didn't understand why Mother would like Jaffar more, who only liked to write calligraphy and read under his favourite tree. Over time, Jaffar spent more time with his mother and Jasmin spent more time with her father. *Well, at least that's what Jasmin thought.*

On the other hand, all Jaffar wanted to do was win his father's love, as he always felt that his father never thought he was good enough at archery. Like his sister, especially after his mother left, he felt lonely. He wanted to win back these artifacts to prove to his Father—and really to himself—that he could do it.

But now, after reading the letter, Jaffar was even angrier. Mother was still alive and she had just—*left*? Mother didn't even explain in the letter why she left or where she had gone, fearing that someone might find the letter.

But, why? Why would she just leave, while everyone thought she was dead?

Nothing made sense anymore. Anger took over Jaffar, as usual. He had trouble bringing the hadith of the Prophet to his mind. He really didn't understand his own anger. Sometimes it would come over him so fast, and he would burst out of control, while other times he could really control it. Jaffar was confused about his Mother's actions. He thought long and hard.

Now, everything is different, thought Jaffar. *I have to win back those artifacts, no matter what.*

"Are you ready, Jaffar?" asked Khan, breaking into Jaffar's thoughts. "It's time for your next mission. You've got to beat the Jannah Jewels in *China*."

"I'm ready," said Jaffar standing up straight, his eyes streaked with red lines, his temples throbbing, and the veins in his arms bulging from holding his bow and arrow so fiercely.

"I am *so* ready," said Jaffar.

3

Caught!

The Jannah Jewels arrived very close to a large body of water in Nanjing, China. Nanjing was an important port, as it was situated along the Yangtze River. It looked as if they had landed right in the middle of a boatyard. There were many large ships and smaller boats docked everywhere. There seemed to be hundreds of people bustling around on the shore, in the ships, on the decks, and all over!

Hidayah and the Jannah Jewels had found a time-travel Maple tree in their favourite neighbourhood park. It was there that Hidayah's Archery Sensei told them about finding 12 artifacts from around the world to place into a Golden Clock to reveal a powerful secret. They

had to travel back into time to find these 12 artifacts that were placed there by the previous Peaceful Archer, before Jaffar and Khan could find them; otherwise the secret could be used for evil. Only the young and animals could travel back into time as a rule set by the Master Archer. This time, Iman's horse, Spirit came through the time travel machine tree too. The Jannah Jewels had already found the first artifact, the manuscript from Mali, Timbuktu.

"Oh no!" cried Jaide. "I dropped my drawing pen in the water. It's my favourite one."

"No problem for me," said Sara, kicking off her flip-flops and dipping into the deep blue, cold waters. She dipped her head under as the pen sank lower and lower. Sara had been swimming since she was a baby. Her parents lived near the ocean, where Sara swam all day long.

"Sara?!" cried Jaide, scanning the waters. "Sara! She's been down there for so long!"

Hidayah readied her bow on her thigh and balanced an arrow on its string. "We'll give her five more seconds and then I'm going to shoot the arrow into the side of that massive ship with this rope attached to it and lower myself into the waters, okay?"

"5-4-3-2-1!" Hidayah released the arrow, and it landed directly into the side of the ship. Hidayah had excellent aim.

Hidayah practiced all day and all night with Sensei Elle. Her favourite part of the day was after practice, when the Sensei and Hidayah would sit together and drink brilliant green tea, sharing in lovely conversation. Hidayah had observed that the green tea wore a shine of its own when she picked it up and gazed upon it in the oil-lamp. It reminded her of the verse in the Qur'an called the Verse of Light, which Hidayah loved to recite:

God is the Light of the Heavens and the Earth.
The parable of His Light is a niche wherein is a lamp—
the lamp is in a glass,
the glass as it were a glittering star—
lit from a blessed olive tree,
neither easterly nor westerly,
whose oil almost lights up,

though fire should not touch it.

Light upon Light.

God guides to His Light whomever He wishes.

God draws parables for mankind,

and God has knowledge of all things.

Sometimes the Sensei and Hidayah would sit together in silence. They had become so close that Hidayah understood what the Sensei needed without her even speaking. Likewise, the Sensei would often answer questions that Hidayah was thinking about without her even asking. Hidayah thought Sensei Elle was a mind reader! But she found out later that anyone could have this ability if they listened more with their hearts and spoke less with their tongues.

Hidayah grabbed the end of the rope and lowered herself deep down into the water.

"Got it!" said Sara bobbing up and down, holding up the drawing pen. "Was there any doubt?"

Hidayah pulled herself back up, gasping to catch her breath. Her hijab was stuck to the side of her head from the water.

"Great swimming, Sara! We can always count on you when it comes to water—*heeey*, what's the big idea?" said Hidayah.

A large net fell into the water and over Hidayah's head! Hidayah's bow was caught on the end and she struggled to free it.

"Look out!" said Iman. Iman gestured to look up. Hidayah, quivering from the cold water, looked up. There in front of her was a huge man with his arms crossed and his eyebrows furrowed, looking right down at Hidayah.

Sara quickly swam over and tried to take the net off Hidayah, but the weight of the net was too heavy in the water. It was one of those nets used to catch large amounts of fish.

Splash! Splish! Splash!

Hidayah struggled with the net.

Whoosh! Splash! Splash!

Finally, Hidayah managed to pull the arrow out of the side of the ship. She used the sharp end of the arrowhead to slice the net, back and forth, back and forth, while she tread water with her legs.

Yes! She did it! Hidayah fell back into the water.

"No, watch out! It's underneath you!" cried Iman.

"These fishermen better not be sport fishing," grumbled Sara. Sara's main purpose in life was to protect the environment. There was nothing that got her angrier than mindless littering and complete unconcern about how the Earth's resources were used or, more like, *squandered*.

Another net swirled around Hidayah as she tried to dodge it this way and that. Like a live fish out of water, she flipped and dipped all around. Sara dived underwater to help save her friend, but as she swam deeper down, the dark, cold waters started to become a little *too* dark for her. She swam back up gasping for air. Sara was an excellent swimmer and could breathe underwater for long periods, but at the same time, she was also afraid of drowning. Hidayah, too exhausted to swim anymore, was scooped up and lifted into the air about twenty feet. It was too late.

"Oh no!" said Sara. "I could've done more to help her."

Sara bobbed up and down in the water, watching as Hidayah was lowered onto the deck of the massive ship.

"That ship must be at least 400-feet long," said Iman, watching with anxious eyes from the shore.

"We've got to do something to help her!" said Jaide.

As Hidayah sat kneeling over, catching her breath, she said a prayer in her heart.

"Please, Allah, grant me an ounce more of energy and strength, just a little bit more."

All of a sudden, Hidayah jolted up. Hidayah had such a powerful and sincere faith that whenever she made a prayer, it was granted instantly. She grabbed her bow and quickly shot her arrow with the rope still tied to it and swung herself over one gigantic mast. The silk sails flapped in the wind. She stood on the top platform, looking victorious, *but not for long*.

"Get down from there!" yelled a one-eyed sailor.

Startled, Hidayah lost her footing and she fell down, down, down from the mast. It must've been at least 100-meters tall.

The Jannah Jewels gasped as they ran toward the ship.

"Gotchya!" said Jaide, as she raced onto the ship and scooped Hidayah up on her skateboard. Then, Jaide sped back towards the gangplank. She was one of the fastest racers, whether on foot or on skateboard, in the world. They came off the ramp and tumbled head first onto the shore.

"Thanks," said Hidayah. She had her hands on her knees, trying to catch her breath.

Sara, meanwhile, had swam back to land. Then, the Jannah Jewels all ran toward a large cluster of cherry blossom trees a little bit farther away from the ships and all the commotion on shore. Luckily, it was so busy that the girls were barely noticed—*at least that's what they thought.*

Hidayah and Sara shivered on the shore behind a big blossom tree, the same tree in which they time-traveled. Jaide and Iman hurried over to meet them. There were hundreds of people on the shore. There were carpenters attending to the ships, cooks bustling back and forth, and traders carrying their goods onto the docks. Children played and ran along the coastline, while others looked on in amazement at this huge fleet of ships.

Jaide pushed on the tree to go back home, but it wouldn't budge. She pushed against it with her hands and feet, still no movement. Meanwhile, Iman walked over and tied a long white bandage around Hidayah's head. Iman loved learning about healing and had learned First Aid so she could help people as well as animals.

"That wooden plank must have hit you hard," said Iman feeling a round bump on Hidayah's forehead.

"Jaide, what are you doing? Stop hurting the tree! It has feelings, too, you know. Besides, we can't go back—we need to find the second artifact," said Sara.

"Hidayah was practically captured just now and you are freezing cold from these waters. There is a gigantic man on one humongous ship who is after us, and there is not a food stall in sight," said Jaide. "This calls for getting out of here!"

The girls sat on the shore and stared back at the silhouette of a tall man on the ship. He was almost two meters tall and looked like he weighed over 200 pounds! He stood with his arms on his hips and his chest out like a warrior.

"He must be the commander of the ship," said Iman.

"Look out!" cried Jaide.

The girls sat distracted by this mysterious man. They turned around just as large nets were thrown on all of them from behind. The girls were carried aboard one of the gigantic ships and dropped onto the deck. They were immediately surrounded from every direction by the ship's armed soldiers and sailors.

4

Aboard the Swimming Dragon

The ship's soldiers lifted the girls out of the nets and set them down on the deck. An echoing gong was heard throughout the bay. The ship's anchor was removed and the ship began to sail, quickly gaining speed on the dark, cold waters. Shouts from the shore could be heard.

"We'll pray for your safe return!" said one.

"Look out for storms!" said another.

"And protect yourself against pirates!" warned another.

"Pirates?" repeated Jaide.

"Where are we?" whispered Sara.

"We are—well, *were* in a boatyard in Nanjing, China," said Iman, reading from the *Book of Knowledge*. "Wait a minute. I can't believe it; can it be?"

"Who, what, where?!" asked Jaide.

"The ship better not be polluting these waters," grumbled Sara.

"Don't worry, Sara, these ships are well-made. If I am right about who this is, we are safe, girls," said Iman.

"Safe? We are in massive trouble," said Sara. "We were just caught in these large fish nets—that are so environmentally a big-no-no for our poor fish—in the middle of China with a big, scary man on this ship!"

"Oh, by the way, here's your pen," said Sara sarcastically, tossing it in the air.

"Gee, thanks for getting it back for me," said Jaide, as she hid inside her hoodie.

Iman kept reading from the *Book of Knowledge*. All of a sudden, she sat straight up.

"I knew it! It's him. It's Ma He!"

"Ma He who?" asked Sara.

"He's better known as Zheng He, the Muslim Admiral

of the Western Seas. He is the commander of this entire fleet," said Iman.

Hidayah reflected for a moment and then spoke with a sparkle in her eye.

"We are in the 15th century!" said Hidayah.

"That's a long time ago!" said Sara. "Look at the amazing knowledge of the people here. The architecture of these ships is just mind-boggling."

"Just look around you. There must be over 300 ships and thousands of men. It's one *huge* fleet," exclaimed Hidayah.

"When I was in the water grabbing *somebody's* pen, I noticed that there were all these eyes painted on the side of the ship," said Sara. "It kind of looks like the ships can *see!*"

"Oh yes, it says here that they were made to look like 'swimming dragons'!" explained Iman. "It was also to ward off any predator ships."

"Ma He, or Zheng He, or whatever, if we're supposed to be safe, why were we inside those large fishing nets as if we were going to be dinner?" said Jaide. "And, are we going to get dinner or what?"

"If we just introduce ourselves, I'm sure he'll be fine with us," said Iman. "Trust me, he probably thinks we are foreign spies listening to where he's going on his next voyage or something."

"What are you thinking we should do?" said Jaide.

"Okay, Jaide, this time you need to be our bridge by speaking in Chinese to the guards," said Iman.

"You want me to ask for food?!" said Jaide happily.

"Nooo!" groaned Iman. "Ask the guards if we can see Zheng He."

"Are you crazy?" asked Jaide.

"Trust me, Jaide," said Iman.

Jaide slowly walked forward. She looked back at Iman, as Iman urged her forward. Jaide straightened her hoodie and went up to one of the men, clearing her throat.

"Excuse me, sir, uhm, yeah. We would like to see Ma He, ah, Zheng He. Uhm, we are not foreign spies. We are Muslims who are trying to help save the world," said Jaide in Chinese.

"Follow me," said one guard. "You'd better be telling the truth."

Iman was already way up ahead, walking alongside the guard. Hidayah followed close by, holding the bandage on her head. Jaide walked sideways, looking front and back. She didn't want someone to throw a net on her again. Sara peeked through all the doors as they walked on the deck.

Through the first window, Sara saw that there were bunk beds; the second window, people were peering over an ancient-looking map and talking with their hands. The third window—yikes! It was Zheng He looking right back into Sara's deep blue eyes.

5

Lightning Strikes

Zheng He came out onto the deck. Iman and Hidayah stood straight and brave. Jaide continued to keep watch behind and above them. As Zheng He approached them, the girls had to bend their heads all the way back to look up at him. He was very tall with big arms the size of baby whales!

"Assalamu'alaykum," said Hidayah, her voice not wavering once. To her relief, Zheng He's face actually relaxed and he smiled.

"Wa alaykum asalaam," he replied with the Muslim greeting. "You must be the Jannah Jewels. You're a lot smaller than those who came before you."

Zheng He spoke in Arabic. Thankfully, Iman could

translate everything. When he was talking to his crew, he switched to talking in Chinese. Then Jaide was able to translate for them.

"Yes, we are the Jannah Jewels. How do you know who we are?" asked Iman.

"I've been expecting you," said Zheng He. "Come now, there is no time to waste. The waters are calm— *for now*."

"*For now*?" gulped Sara.

"Come in and have something to eat," said Zheng He. The girls followed him down to the second level of the ship, while the ship sped along the dark, cold waters.

"Yes! Finally! Now you're talking! What do we have here? Noodles, fish, buns, veggies. Excuse me, coming through, don't mind if I do," said Jaide, already gobbling down her food. The entire second level of the ship was dedicated to food. There were all kinds of goodies to eat, as well as cooks, kitchens, stoves, ovens, tables, chairs, people coming and going, and people eating and drinking.

The other three girls joined Jaide and Zheng He for some lunch on the second level, while they listened to booming thunder overhead.

CRASH! BOOM!

Thunder shouted in the skies. After ten seconds, lightning followed and the whole sky lit up like fireworks on 'Eid day. The waves lurked like a great white shark looking for prey.

6

The Man with the White Mask

Piercing rain and stinging hailstones came pounding down onto the upper deck. Everyone starting running around—the doctors, the scribes, the shipbuilders, and the cooks.

Members of the crew secured the great white sails that looked like cumulous clouds. Zheng He took hold of the gigantic steering wheel as they lurched on the open waters. Warning beats came from drums, flags ripped in the wind, and bells sounded faint against the raging waters.

"I wonder what fleet this is," said Iman. "Zheng He is famous for going on seven amazing expeditions. On each of his voyages he went to different places and traded goods with the people there. On one journey to East Africa, he brought back a zebra for China!"

CRASH! BOOM!

"I have visited many places, you are right. In this fleet, we are going to my friend's port in Malacca."

"Where is Malacca?" asked Jaide.

"Malacca is in Southeast Asia," replied Zheng He.

Hidayah peered over the ancient map she took from the tree. There it was in bold letters:

Artifact #2

Medicinal Plant

Malacca, Southeast Asia

Hidayah hid under an alcove, so the rain wouldn't ruin the map. To her right was a large cargo box. She looked inside. There were hollow bamboo poles in it.

"May I have a bamboo pole?" asked Hidayah.

"Sure, help yourself," said Zheng He. He was an admiral also known for his generosity.

Hidayah took the bamboo pole and a knife and carved out the inside, making it smooth, and then cut the bamboo about a hand's length. She blew into the hole to remove any extra dust from the carving. Then, she cut a long straight and thin bamboo, like string, and clasped it on either side of the container.

"Brilliant, Hidayah!" said Iman.

Hidayah rolled up the map and slipped it inside her new map bamboo container. She slipped the long, straight, thin bamboo string over her shoulder. It stayed snug to her body.

"Now it won't get wet," said Hidayah. "Our next mission is to find a special medicinal plant and bring it back to the tree before time runs out!"

"Time?" Jaide checked her time-travel watch. "We don't have much of it!"

Hidayah thought back to the time-travel tree to remember the Sensei's warning.

"*You have to find the sacred plant that will help the disease of blindness," said the Sensei. "Remember, you must complete the mission before time runs out or you will be stuck here forever!*"

The girls were given jobs on the ship during the journey to Malacca. Iman helped Zheng He read the navigation maps, while Jaide helped keep the decks dry by tying cloths to the end of her skateboard. Hidayah helped steer the ship, while Sara helped measure the distance travelled with the ship's speedometer. The ship rocked back and forth on the giant waves. The girls shivered in the rain.

"That's mine, give it back!" the one-eyed sailor cried out. He and another sailor were arguing over something in the boxes of cargo. One man was wearing a strange white mask, while the other was wearing an eye patch. Hidayah hid behind a few cargo boxes, so she wouldn't be seen. Suddenly, she saw a large, long shadow on the wall. It was being raised by one of the sailors. It looked like a sword, or maybe it was a gun, or maybe it was—

WHACK!

7

Pirates!

Hidayah jumped up on top of the cargo box just in time. The long stick was one of the bamboo poles used to carry water. The copper bowl on one end swung wildly from side to side as the man with the white mask tried to hit Hidayah with it.

WHACK!

A waft of fresh fish encircled Hidayah. The man with the white mask had knocked over a huge cargo box of fish while trying to get Hidayah. The smell was so strong, Hidayah had to cover her nose with her hijab. Suddenly, Hidayah felt a tug at her neck.

SQUAK! SQUAK! SQUAK!

Seagulls came swooping down and all around.

Hidayah tried to wave them away with her arms and hands. The seagulls landed nearby, pecking at the banquet of fish all over the floor. Meanwhile, the man with the white mask had vanished. The one-eyed sailor was running off down the starboard of the ship.

"Oh no, the map," said Hidayah looking down at her shirt. It was gone!

Jaide came rolling by with towels still stuck to her skateboard, sending a flutter of seagulls back into the sky.

"What's with all the seagulls? What happened?" asked Jaide, looking at all the remaining fish.

"These sailors were fighting, and then the seagulls came squawking, and my map—it's gone!"

All of a sudden, the man with the white mask jumped out of a cargo box as the lid went crashing down. Instinctively, Jaide sped towards him at top speed, knocking him off his feet. Hidayah readied the bow and held the arrowhead a few inches from the man's white mask. Around his neck was Hidayah's bamboo container, which held the ancient map.

"Remove the mask and show yourself!"

The sailor didn't move.

"I said remove the mask, right now," said Hidayah. "Give me back my map!"

Jaide rolled by and scooped down to grab the bamboo container from the man with the white mask.

Thunder boomed and a large flash of lightning lit up the sky.

"Don't look directly at it," cried Iman.

Everybody fell over onto the deck as the ship rocked aggressively back and forth. The man with the white mask took his chance while Hidayah was off balance. He pushed her aside as the ship continued to rock. He ran down the starboard and jumped right into the water!

SSPLAASSH!

Hidayah and Jaide ran after him and looked down and across the water. They couldn't believe what they saw.

"Pirates!" cried Jaide.

The ship tossed in the waters while shark-like waves crashed up against the sides. The wind howled as day turned into night.

A single pirate boat cut through the waters, moving rather quickly towards Zheng He's ship. It picked up the man in the white mask as waves splashed higher and higher and Zheng He's ship rocked violently, throwing people and boxes all over.

The man swung himself onto the boat and slowly removed his mask.

"It's Jaffar!" said Hidayah.

"How did he find us?" said Sara.

All of a sudden, arrows with fiery tips came flaming across the dark waters onto the ship's deck. The girls quickly gathered around with buckets of water and made an assembly line as Zheng He's army took their places. They all knew exactly what to do. The flaming arrows were put out as soon as they hit the ship. Zheng He's army was too many for Jaffar and the pirates.

"You will be defeated," boomed Zheng He with confidence. "You must surrender or you will be wiped out by the storm *and* my army."

"I will never surrender to you!" cried Jaffar. More flaming arrows were shot through the sky, landing on the ship. But Zheng He proved to be a fierce admiral.

46

He fought against Jaffar and the pirates diligently.

"You will never get the artifacts, Jaffar!" cried Iman.

Jaffar's eyes were red, angry, and puffy as he stared at Hidayah. All of a sudden, one large flaming arrow was sent across the sky.

"Watch out!"

Hidayah fell over as Iman pushed her out of the way. The arrow hit Iman on her arm.

Zheng He steered the ship away from Jaffar, and because his ship was so big, large waves from its wake came crashing down on the pirate's small ships.

CRACK!

Lightning struck a tall mast of Zheng He's ship. The silk sails came loose, flapping wildly in the wind. Crewmembers hammered hard to fix the mast as the rain continued to pour down like elephants and giraffes. The mast could not hold any longer. It teetered down right towards them.

8

Drowning

Jaide threw a big rope to Iman, who grabbed hold. Jaide rolled up to Iman, and then grabbed Sara and Hidayah and placed them all on the skateboard, reaching one side of the ship.

CRAAAA-AAASH!

The tall mast fell down with a large bang, just missing the Jannah Jewels. All of a sudden, Jaide lost hold of the rope. She went tumbling off her skateboard and fell down with a thump before the mast.

"Jaide!" yelled Hidayah. She ran back to her and dragged her over to the other girls.

KKKRRRK!

Two girls were now wounded and there was still a long way to go. The storm seemed unending, but they had a mission to complete, and the Jannah Jewels were going to complete it—*no matter what.*

KKKRRRK!

The girls watched with wide eyes, huddled in a corner, while Jaffar's ship cracked. His ship began to dip below the waters. It was sinking fast.

Suddenly, a beautiful verse from the Holy Qur'an came to Hidayah's mind,

"Goodness and evil can never be equal..."

"Jaffar!" cried Hidayah.

"I thought he was your enemy?" said Zheng He.

"He just threw flaming arrows at us. A person like that doesn't need to be helped," said a sailor.

"He's right, you're out of your mind," said another.

All of a sudden, a large wave came and hit Jaffar over the head. He disappeared under the dark, deep waters.

"Nooooo!" screamed Hidayah.

"*Repel evil with what is better...*" the verses continued.

Hidayah ran over to Zheng He's lifeboats that were positioned in a row alongside the ship. She climbed up the mast quickly and cut the rope. Down came one lifeboat. Zheng He watched and decided to help. He steered the great ship in such a way that a large wave was created to push the lifeboat over to Jaffar.

Zheng He pulled the ship back on course, while Hidayah and the Jannah Jewels watched from a distance. Hidayah's eyes darted back and forth scanning the waters.

"It's too late, Hidayah," said Jaide. She put her arms around Hidayah. Hidayah pulled away with large teardrops falling from her eyes like round beads from an abacus. She kept scanning the waters.

All of a sudden, Jaffar's head appeared, like a great white shark jumping out of the water for a moment to catch a fish. His friend grabbed him out of the water and quickly pulled him into the boat. Meanwhile, the Qur'anic verse continued to play in Hidayah's head:

"*Then see: the one between whom and you there*

was enmity has become a good friend."

Jaffar's head was down, his hair dripping as he gasped for breath. Hidayah stared and stared. Finally, he looked up. His eyes were now tired and weary. He looked at Hidayah with a hint of confusion and sadness in his eyes. Jaffar wondered why she would help him, and Hidayah wondered the same.

It is what my Sensei would have done, thought Hidayah.

"Time is running out!" cried Jaide interrupting Hidayah's thoughts. "I don't know if we're going to make it, Jannah Jewels."

Jaide fell back onto the ship completely exhausted, while the ship pressed on cutting through the waves with a full moon illuminating the way.

9

Pirate Bait

Slowly, Jaide's eyes began to flicker open. She had to use her hand to shield the blazing rays of the sun.

It must be just past noon, thought Jaide, observing the height of the sun.

She moved her other hand across the floor. Her hands felt something smooth, soft, and silky, different than the rough, coarse, and rugged floor of Zheng He's 'swimming dragon' ships. Jaide slowly pulled herself up to a sitting position. She gingerly touched her head. Everything seemed to be spinning. As her eyes began to focus, she couldn't believe what she saw.

It was SAND!

"Yes! We made it onto land!" she cried. Jaide looked

all around.

"Girls?" she called. "Iman? Hidayah! SARA!"

There was no answer.

Jaide rubbed her head again. She had taken a big fall on that ship. She looked right, then left. There were rows and rows of trees, bushes, and tall grass. Malacca had miles and miles of sand for as far as she could see. Spotting Zheng He's ship anchored by the shore about twenty-five meters away was a relief. People were still bustling back and forth on the ship like they were back at the port in Nanjing, China.

I am so hungry, thought Jaide. Her lips were chapped and parched. She spotted a trail of footsteps leading into the island and decided to follow them. Plants and vines hung in every direction as she walked on the trail, following the footsteps. She stopped to examine some round berries on the bushes to see if they were edible. She picked them one by one and dropped them into her backpack.

I'd better ask Iman about them, just in case they are poisonous, thought Jaide, *even though I could eat all of them right now.* She resisted popping one or two into her mouth for as long as she could. She could just imagine the juice that would burst into her mouth. Finally, she couldn't resist any longer. She popped one into her mouth. Bright red juice squirted from her face. She soured her face a little bit, but then she swallowed them. *Hmm, not so bad, but I better wait to eat the rest.* She turned and continued along the trail.

"Saaaaraaa," she called into the silence.

Suddenly, the ground beneath her feet was swept from underneath her. It was a net!

"Oh no, not again!" cried Jaide. "It's a day of nets for the Jannah Jewels!"

The net scooped her up and tightly pulled around her. She was flung into the air into a very tall tree.

Jaide struggled and wriggled and tried to stand up. Hanging in the air, she started to feel nauseous. She leaned her body all to one side of the net and then to the other side. She began to slowly swing back and forth, back and forth in the net. Finally, she was swinging so fast, she was able to swing the net into a large tree branch beside her. She sat in the net, in the tree, exhausted. Everything around her started to spin again. She closed her eyes to try to make it stop. Her head started to pound. She opened her eyes and looked around her. She could still see the ship and the water. But what was that at the far end of the island? She squinted and shaded her eyes from the sun. It was a lifeboat from Zheng He's ship. *That's odd*, she thought. Then she looked closer at the boat. It looked very familiar, more than just being Zheng He's boat.

"Wait a minute!" said Jaide. A large cluster of birds flew away at the sound of her voice.

This is the lifeboat that Jaffar climbed into last night in the storm! He must be on the island and I'm pretty sure some of his pirate friends will be here too, she thought. *How am I going to warn the others without getting into deeper trouble?*

"Look it here, boys, we have found some bait!" said Jaffar, looking up at Jaide.

"I knew it!" said Jaide, looking below her. "Let me go!" Jaide began throwing the hard red berries at Jaffar.

"Tell me where the Golden Clock is hidden," shouted Jaffar.

"No way. You can put me in nets or whatever—I will

not tell you," said Jaide still throwing berries at Jaffar and his gang. "Never."

"Hidayah doesn't know that I have built my strength in the last few years. I have trained hard. She looks weak to me. The Golden Clock and the artifacts will be mine," said Jaffar wickedly. "Don't you know that girls don't become heirs to thrones? At least, not without a good fight."

His gang laughed out loud. Jaide struggled in the net. She threw more berries and finally, one hit Jaffar right in his eye! Jaffar and the gang stopped laughing, while Jaffar shrieked out in pain.

"Hidayah will win in the next archery battle because she is stronger than you. And the Jannah Jewels will find the next artifact before you, Jaffar, you'll see," said Jaide.

Jaffar turned to his gang squinting. "Throw her in the ocean. No, better yet, leave her here. She can't do anything while being stuck in a tree, and the wild animals will eventually come out at night," he cackled. "Let's follow this trail. Hidayah is close by—I smell victory!"

10

The Ring of Fire

"I wonder how much longer we have to solve this mystery. I sure hope Jaide is all right," said Sara.

"Don't worry, Sara. Jaide will be fine. She needs to rest after hurting her head on the ship. I'm glad we have finally made it to Malacca," said Iman.

"Malacca is a destination where we usually stop to repair our ships, rest, and trade some goods. We are going to get things back in order and set out once again," said Zheng He.

Hidayah opened up the map. "According to this map, the next artifact is right here in Malacca. We have to find it before Zheng He sets out back on the ocean," said Hidayah. There it was—an image of a small plant in Southeast Asia—the second artifact.

"The plant is here. We just have to keep looking," said Iman. "We will find it. We have to."

"Yes, the plant you are looking for could be here. It grows in unusual places, and nobody knows why. That is why the plant is so special and rare. Legend says that only the people who are supposed to find it, do. Otherwise, it makes itself unknown to people. But that's for you to find out," said Zheng He.

"I hope we are those people it will make itself known to," said Hidayah.

"You know, I was wondering, have we been traveling long?" asked Sara.

"In a way, yes, and in a way, no. In time-travel, anything can happen," said Iman.

"What do you mean? Haven't we been away from Canada for a really long time?" asked Sara.

"No, whenever we go on an adventure, time stands still in Canada for us. We come back at exactly the same time as we left. Even if we travel for a really long time in an adventure, like this one, we always get back in the same year we left, on the exact same day, at the exact hour," said Hidayah.

"That's a relief because we don't want to age when we are barely even teenagers," said Sara, passing around the sunscreen. "Here, put this on. It will protect you from the UV rays."

"Okay, you two go on ahead and try to find this plant. I'm going to go back and check on Jaide. She probably woke up hungry and is wondering where we all went," said Iman.

Iman climbed onto Spirit's back.

"Don't worry. I will get Jaide and come right back," said Iman.

Iman sped down the trails with her hijab flapping in the wind behind her.

"You forgot to say, inshaAllah," Sara called after her. "That means she won't come *right* back, will she?"

"InshaAllah," said Hidayah. "InshaAllah, she'll come back with Jaide."

Hidayah and Sara kept walking. "This place is so big. How are we ever going to find this plant?" said Sara.

They climbed over tall grass and deep sand pits, tripped over vines, and inched their way through mud. It seemed like they had been walking for hours.

Iman and Jaide should've been back by now, thought Sara.

Hidayah and Sara were exhausted from the heat of the sun. Water was running out and the plant couldn't be seen anywhere.

Hidayah took out her ancient compass and started fiddling around with it. It was a neat-looking compass. Sara looked at her metal ball and threw it up in the air. She had no idea what it was for.

"Please Allah, you are ar-Rahman, ar-Rahim. Please help us find the plant and let us get back safely to Canada," said Hidayah.

Nothing happened. Several minutes passed. Hidayah lay back onto the grass.

"I still don't get why I got this metal ball. It doesn't seem to do anything at all," said Sara. She tossed it up in the air and caught it a couple of times more.

"Let me see it," said Hidayah. She examined it a

little closer.

"Look at all these intricate designs on it," said Hidayah. "Did you notice that? It probably means something. I wonder what those little round circles are for?"

"Great, it's not just a metal ball, but it's a *fancy* metal ball," said Sara sarcastically.

Sara kept rotating the metal ball in her hands, while Hidayah kept her eyes closed, waiting for the familiar feeling in her heart. Hidayah had practiced for a very long time with the Sensei on how to still her heart. It was only through stilling her heart that she was able to pray to God and have anything she asked for come true. Sometimes, when her heart wasn't still, her prayers took longer to be answered. Hidayah remembered the Sensei telling her that to still the heart, one should pray. Hidayah tried again.

But, still nothing happened.

Frustrated, Hidayah sat back down and tried to clear her heart. Sara was mumbling something to Hidayah.

"Sssshhh!" said Hidayah. "I can't concentrate."

Sara looked away.

"Sorry, Sara," said Hidayah. "I guess I'm just exhausted from this trip and we might be running out of time. We have to go back and find Jaide and check the time-travel watch. And where is Iman? She should have been back by now."

"A minute ago, you told me to stop worrying," said Sara. "Now, it's your turn. Remember the words of the Sensei, *'Hidayah, whenever you ask, you must ask with your heart.'*"

"Yes, that's it!" said Hidayah. This time Hidayah went into *sujud*, prostration into the grass beside her, and again asked God for His help.

You are the closest to God when you are in sujud, she remembered the Sensei's voice.

At last, the feeling came to her heart. She grabbed the ancient compass and pointed it towards the South. She and Sara ran across a big grassy field. They jogged along for a few minutes and at last they came to a large pond. And there, in the middle of the pond on a big lily pad was an amazingly vibrant plant that looked like no other.

"This is the plant. It's right here on the ancient map," exclaimed Hidayah.

The pond was deep and covered with lily pads and vines. It would take an expert swimmer to get to the plant and Sara was just the girl for the job. She kicked off her flip-flops and climbed in. She dodged vines and swam under branches all the way to the middle of the pond. When she approached the special plant, she grabbed hold of the entire lily pad. She started to swim back with the whole thing.

While swimming, Sara recalled some information that Iman had shared with her on the ship. Iman had read from the *Book of Knowledge* that the scientist Al-Idrisi made major contributions in the 11th century to the science of medicinal plants and wrote several books, too. He reviewed all the medicinal plants known to different Muslim scientists and added to it his own research collection from his travels. It is due to scientists like Al-Idrisi and other famous scholars that Muslims were among the first scientific healers because of their tremendous research and knowledge.

Sara looked up to see Hidayah smiling back at her.

"*Be grateful and I will give you more*," Hidayah remembered another verse from the Qur'an.

Hidayah went back to bowing down, in *sujud*, thanking Allah for helping all of them once again.

Sara swam with one hand on the plant while the other hand moved logs out of her way.

Hidayah was anxiously waving to Sara to hurry back. Suddenly, Spirit, Iman's horse, came racing towards them, but it was not Iman on Spirit's back—

It was Jaffar!

"We meet again, eh, Hidayah?" said Jaffar. Sara ducked behind a log in the water. She had to tread water in order to say afloat. She did so quietly, so she wouldn't attract attention to herself.

The bamboo pole, the one Hidayah had made for the map, shone in the sun around Hidayah's neck. Hidayah readied her bow and arrow. Jaffar, seated on Spirit's back, anxiously circled around her, with his bow and arrow ready, too.

"Where are my friends?" said Hidayah.

"Give me the map. Or better yet, tell me where the

Golden Clock is and I will give you back your friends *alive*," said Jaffar.

"We will not tell you about the Golden Clock," said Hidayah.

"Then say goodbye to your little friends," said Jaffar.

The pirates that were helping Jaffar pushed Jaide and Iman forward. They fell to the ground. Hidayah saw that their hands were tied and cloths were in their mouths.

"Let them go!" said Hidayah.

Suddenly, Spirit saw Iman and neighed wildly. Spirit raced towards Iman, knocking Jaffar off. Spirit reached Iman safely, gently nudging her.

Meanwhile, Hidayah ran up to Jaffar while he was down and held the arrow close to his nose.

"You don't have the guts," said Jaffar. "You saved me in the water for who-knows-what reason. You were always *too* nice Hidayah. Nice just doesn't cut it for the next Master Archer. You must be fierce to be the next heir to the throne."

"Last time I checked, anger doesn't get you

anywhere," said Hidayah.

Jaffar tried to get up, but Hidayah's arrow was too close to him.

"Don't you remember a time when there was balance on the Earth, when all the Masters defended the Earth against evil?" said Hidayah.

Just then, Sara climbed out of the water with the medicinal plant. Jaffar's eyes grew wide at the sight of it. With all of his strength, Jaffar pushed Hidayah down. He snapped his fingers. Pirates threw flaming arrows all around Hidayah. She was trapped in a ring of fire three-feet high.

"Now who is victorious?" said Jaffar. "Ha ha ha!"

Hidayah's arm bled from a cut of one of the pirates'arrows. She placed her other hand on top of it. Suddenly, Hidayah's compass twinkled in the sunlight.

"The ancient compass," said Jaffar. He reached out for it, but the flames were too high and much too hot for him. He squealed in pain at his burning hand. His plan worked against him.

"Your own anger will destroy you," said Hidayah

from behind the flames. "It doesn't have to be like this."

Jaffar fell back onto the ground, rolling around in pain from the burning fire.

Meanwhile, Sara slipped the plant into her bag and ran back to Jaide and Iman, untying them. Iman climbed onto Spirit, while Jaide raced back on her skateboard with Sara.

"Okay, Spirit, I know you can do it," said Iman. She sped towards the ring of fire. And at last, as she reached the edge, she pulled the reins up and Spirit jumped right over the ring of fire!

Hidayah jumped on and held on tight as Spirit gathered up speed and jumped back over the ring of fire. Jaffar covered his eyes from the ashy flames Spirit had kicked up from the ground. The pirates tried to run after them, but Zheng He and the Malaccan army had found them and surrounded them on all sides. The girls were free as they raced back to the ships. A commanding boom came from Zheng He's treasure ship.

"Nooooo!" cried Jaffar, pounding his good hand into the sand.

"Yes! We got the plant," said Hidayah, reaching the

ship.

"Well done," said Zheng He.

"We must go back to Nanjing and back to the Chinese blossom tree," said Iman. "We can not continue this voyage with you. We have what we came for."

"I will return with you, Jannah Jewels, to the land of China so I can see you off safely," said Zheng He.

The big cloud-like sails filled with wind and the giant ship began its journey back to China.

"What will Jaffar do next?" asked Iman.

"He will not give up. I saw real anger in him today. Jaffar has his own time travel tree that his Father built. The Sensei told me that he built it with a scientist who knew the Master Archer. I have to be ready for him," said Hidayah. "He will be back."

11

Time's Running Out

The sun shone through yesterday's ominous, dark clouds. The girls all tumbled back into their ship's quarters, exhausted from the fight. Iman nursed Hidayah's bleeding arm and lay her down in one of the many bunk beds for rest. Soon Hidayah fell asleep, but with one hand resting on her bamboo pole.

The others climbed to the upper deck of the ship. The waters were shining bright. They sailed for what seemed like a long time.

"We have exactly fifteen minutes to get back to the tree," said Jaide sitting up.

"Don't worry, we will be there in time," said Zheng He.

The girls watched as the shore came closer and closer. Jaide's eyes kept darting from her watch to the shore, from the shore to her watch.

"Can't this ship go any faster?" she said. "We have only six minutes left."

The ship finally reached shore. The girls turned to say "Salam" to Zheng He, while the sailors unloaded old supplies and reloaded new ones. Jaide and Sara raced off the ship on the skateboard. Iman and Hidayah jumped on Spirit.

As Spirit ran across the ship, all of a sudden, she stopped at the ramp and didn't want to get off. Spirit neighed strangely and kicked up her front legs in self-defence. As Spirit kicked up her front legs, Hidayah's backpack with the plant slid off her shoulder, and down it fell.

"Oh no, the plant!" cried Hidayah. She watched closely with her super eyesight to see where the bag fell. It landed in a cargo box pile that sailors were already carrying onto the shore.

"What is it?" Iman asked Spirit. "Everything okay?" She listened closely to Spirit's heart with her gift of being able to communicate with animals.

"There's something under the ramp," she said.

Meanwhile, Hidayah jumped down to the cargo boxes. All the boxes looked exactly the same. She looked inside each one. "Silk and porcelain," said Hidayah. "Not here. Gold and silverware, copper utensils, and iron—nope, not here either."

"Two minutes!"

"Live animals, no, live fish. No, not here either," cried Hidayah.

"Please Allah, help us find my backpack with the plant!"

"Pirates!" screamed Iman. "Underneath the ramp, stealing cargo!"

Zheng He came right away with his armed soldiers.

"Not in my home, they don't!" Zheng He's army took up their positions. But the girls couldn't wait to see the outcome. They had to leave immediately.

"I have the plant!" said Hidayah, waving it over her head.

"Lucky for us, Spirit knew something was wrong,"

said Sara.

"Animals sense danger way before we humans do," said Iman.

"Ten seconds!" cried out Jaide.

The girls raced to the tree. Breathing rapidly, they all pushed the blossom tree. They heard a familiar clickety-clack, and down, down, down they went, sliding through the tunnel.

They all joined hands and repeated the phrase, "*Bismillah-irRahman-irRahim!*"

They heard a great whirring sound and when they opened their eyes, they found themselves in a familiar place in a familiar time.

12

Master Swimmer

"Well, girls, I don't know about you, but that was one big adventure," said Jaide.

"You're back, and with the plant, I hope?" said a voice from behind the shadows. It was Sensei Elle, but there was another person with her. She was wearing flowing, sky blue robes.

"I am the Master Swimmer. I work with the other Masters. Sara, you showed great skill in the waters. You are fast becoming an excellent apprentice."

The Jannah Jewels looked on in amazement. Sara beamed.

"Thank you," said Sara.

Hidayah gave Sara the plant. Sara walked over

to the Golden Clock and bent down on her hands and knees. She found the hour for two o'clock and placed the plant inside. It was a perfect fit as the walls and the tree glowed with the new puzzle piece in place.

"Congratulations, Jannah Jewels, you have proven yourselves once again," said Sensei Elle. "Your training will become more intense and you will face even more challenges in the coming adventures."

"Jaffar is getting angrier," said Hidayah.

"Yes, but you showed great leadership when you chose to spare his life in the waters," said Master Swimmer. "It is a mark of a great Master on her way."

"Farewell, until next time." And they both disappeared.

Hidayah rolled the ancient map back up into the bamboo container.

The girls looked at the Wall of Secrets again. There was Hidayah's Sensei next to the Master Swimmer they had just met.

"I have a feeling we are going to meet the other two people in this picture very soon," said Hidayah.

"But not anytime soon!" cried Jaide. "Let's go! No more flaming arrows or nets capturing us. Anybody for peanut butter and banana sandwiches?"

"Wouldn't mind it at all, actually," said Hidayah.

The girls laughed as they walked home in the glorious sun still thinking about their close call with Jaffar.

Will Jaffar get even closer next time? Will Hidayah be able to defend herself against Jaffar's growing anger? Will the girls be able to help Hidayah?

Find out in the next adventure, "Bravery in Baghdad," with more clues to the mystery of the Golden Clock.

Don't miss the next Jannah Jewels book!

In the third book, a notable scholar has vanished from the House of Wisdom, along with a scroll pen that belonged to the famous mathematician Al-Kindi.

Lost in the marketplace of Baghdad, can the Jannah Jewels gain victory over the villain and put the pen back into the Golden Clock?

Find out more about the third book by visiting our website at

www.JannahJewels.com

Glossary

Alhamdulillahi Rabbil Alameen: "All praise is due to God" in Arabic. This prayer is said when thankful of something or to show appreciation.

Allah: It is a word that means God in Arabic.

Assalamu'alaykum: "May the peace of God be with you" in Arabic.

BismillahirRahmanirRaheem: "In the name of God, Most Gracious, Most Merciful" in Arabic. This prayer is said before beginning something one has intended.

Hadith: a saying from the Prophet Muhammad, peace and blessings be upon him

Hijab: a head-scarf or literally in Arabic it means to cover

InshaAllah: "If it is God's will" in Arabic. It is said when indicating hope for something to occur in the future.

Jannah: heaven, paradise or garden

Qur'an: The central religious text of Muslims. Muslims believe it is the word of God as revealed to Prophet Muhammad, peace and blessings be upon him, through the Arch Angel Gabriel.

SubhanAllah: "Glorious is God" in Arabic. This prayer is said when in awe of something.

Sujud: prostration, a position in the Islamic prayer where the head is lowered to the ground

Walaikum asalaam: "May the peace of God be upon you too" in Arabic and is said in response when greeted with Assalamu'alaykum

To find out more about our other books,

go to:

www.JannahJewels.com

63241761R00056

Made in the USA
Lexington, KY
01 May 2017